There's Nothing Wrong

Written by Jo Cotterill

Illustrated by Mark Sweeney

Collins

Chapter 1

When Mum got ill, I wasn't worried to start with. She was a sporty person – always had loads of energy and was never too busy to kick a ball around the garden with me. She ate lots of fruit and vegetables – way more than five a day. I thought she'd get better really quickly.

But she didn't. On Day Three, she was so tired, she couldn't even get up from the sofa, and she kept coughing. I said, "Maybe you need some fresh air," but Mum didn't seem to have enough breath even to finish a sentence, let alone stand up. She rang the doctor, but the advice was just to stay home and rest.

Something you need to know about me: I love football. Not like it. I *love* it. I don't know why, that's just how it is. I practise in the garden every day, and most days Mum comes too. She's pretty good in goal. Playing footie is something we've done together for years. When she got ill, I had to practise on my own, and it wasn't as much fun.

"Will *you* play football with me?" I asked my older brother Jonny.

"No," said Jonny. "I'm watching videos. Go away, Harry."

So, I went back outside and started some keepy-uppies.

On Day Four, Dad came to pick up me and Jonny.

Mum smiled weakly and gave us feeble hugs and said, "Don't worry. I just need to rest up. Dad will look after you while I get better. It won't be long."

As we drove away, *that* was when I started to worry. That moment right there. Mum had *never* been too sick to look after us before. I clutched Bear as we drove to Dad's house. Don't laugh. I'm not ashamed of having a bear. I bet you have one too.

Dad was nice. He lived with Marie, who was nice too. But neither of them understood me like Mum did. When Mum called me in for dinner, she understood if I didn't come in straight away because I was in the middle of a keepy-uppy. Dad got annoyed if I didn't appear at the back door within ten seconds.

"Harry, dinner will get cold if you don't come when I call," Dad told me, frowning.

I stared down at my plate of fish fingers, beans and chips, and felt a bit sick.

"I'm not hungry," I said.

"You need the energy," Dad told me, "for your football!" He smiled at me, but I felt like there was something wriggly in my tummy. Something that didn't leave any room for food.

I found it hard to go to sleep at Dad's too. I lay awake in the dark, staring at the ceiling and wondering how Mum was. Jonny came crashing in when it was his time to go to bed, waking me up again. Sometimes I heard him and Dad arguing: "It's way past your bedtime!" Dad would say, and Jonny would retort, "I go to bed later at Mum's." Then Dad would snap, "Well, you're not at Mum's now!"

Several days went past and whenever I asked Dad how Mum was, he said, "She's doing OK, Harry. It's a nasty illness. She sends her love."

"When will we be going home?"

"Soon."

I asked Jonny if I could call Mum on his phone. He rolled his eyes and sighed. "I'm in the middle of something." I tried calling from Dad's phone, but Mum didn't answer.

It was so hard not knowing how Mum was. What if she was really, really sick, all on her own and nobody knew? I clutched Bear tighter to me and tried to pretend everything was OK.

Chapter 2

Jonny and I stayed with Dad and Marie for two weeks. It was nice to spend more time with Dad, but I was so looking forward to seeing Mum again. When we finally went home, I hugged her and didn't want to let go.

"Come and sit down with me," she said eventually. "I can't stand up for very long yet."

Jonny ran upstairs to his room and immediately plugged into his video games. Mum and I hugged on the sofa.

"Are you better?" I asked.

She kissed my head. "I'm much better than I was. But I'm still not properly well, Harry. It's very annoying." She stopped to catch her breath. "There are lots of things I want to do, and I just haven't got the energy. Nan and Grandad are coming in every few days to help with food and cleaning and things like that."

"OK," I said. "Do you think Grandad could play football with me?"

"I'm sure he could," said Mum with a smile.

The next morning, we got up for school but Mum didn't get dressed.

"Jonny's going to walk you in this morning," she told me. "And Sam from next door said she'll bring you home at the end of school. Just for a few days, while I get more energy."

Oh. "OK," I said, but I was disappointed. I kind of thought everything would go back to normal when we came home.

Walking in with Jonny wasn't the same. He walks really fast, and he listens to music on his phone, so he didn't talk to me on the way. He dropped me at the bottom of the school driveway and said, "See ya." Before I could reply, he'd gone. I walked up the driveway on my own, feeling a bit … well. Empty.

Sam's daughter Cassie was in the year below me, and she talked a *lot*. So, on the way into school, I wished someone would talk to me, and on the way home, I wished they wouldn't! Mum always met me at the door, smiling, still pale and tired, still in her dressing gown. Sometimes Nan and Grandad were there too and that was great because Grandad was always up for a game of footie, and it made me feel loads better.

"You deserve a treat," Nan said to me and Jonny after school on Friday. "We're taking you to the milkshake shop."

"Brilliant!" I said. I love the milkshake shop. It has 37 flavours of milkshake, and you can have any chocolate bar or sweets whizzed up into it. My two favourite flavours are gingerbread and green apple. Not together, of course – yuck! Jonny likes sour cherry, raspberry and pistachio. Mum's favourite is mocha. She always has a mocha milkshake with dark chocolate whizzed into it. I ran to tell her. "Mum! Mum, we're going to the milkshake shop!"

She was still on the sofa, still in her dressing gown. I stopped short. "Aren't you coming?"

She smiled at me, but her forehead was still creased, like it so often was these days. "I'm sorry, Harry, I wish I could. Will you bring me back my favourite?"

I felt so disappointed. "Why can't you come? Nan's going to drive us. It's not far to walk from the car park to the shop. And you could sit down when you're there."

14

Mum looked at me for a moment, and then she said, "All right. Give me a moment to get dressed, OK? Tell Nan and Grandad to wait for me."

Happiness bubbled up inside me. "Nan!" I yelled. "Mum's coming!"

Nan appeared in the doorway, frowning. "I don't think that's a very good idea, Kelly. You're meant to be resting."

"I do nothing *but* rest," Mum said, pushing herself up off the sofa with an effort. "Harry wants me to come, so I'm coming."

"Yessss!" I punched the air. "I'll help you up the stairs, Mum."

She had to pause at the top to catch her breath again and rolled her eyes at me. "I still get so frustrated! When will I get better?"

"You have to be patient," I told her. "One day at a time."

I *loved* having Mum with us at the milkshake shop. It was the first time she'd left the house in three weeks. *Three weeks*! She had her mocha milkshake and enjoyed it, and Jonny told us a rude joke he'd heard at school and Nan gasped and said it wasn't appropriate for me to hear, but I didn't understand it and no one would explain it to me. I didn't care though because Mum was out and smiling and even though she looked very white and kept coughing, she was here and so everything was fine.

And then we got home, and she collapsed onto the sofa and didn't stop coughing for half an hour and Nan sent her to bed.

"It's all my fault," I said to Nan. "Isn't it? I made her come to the shop."

Nan hugged me. "It's not your fault, Harry. It's just this nasty illness."

But my stomach felt so awful that my milkshake got confused and came back up the wrong way. I didn't think I'd ever want gingerbread flavour again.

Chapter 3

Mum had to stay in bed for a whole week after the milkshake shop visit. Nan and Grandad came round nearly every day to clean the house or mow the lawn or put me to bed. Mum couldn't even read to me because she didn't have enough breath. It was … horrible.

"Why can't the doctor do anything?" I asked her.

Mum hugged me. "I know how you feel, Harry. There's nothing anyone can do. My illness was caused by a virus, and even when the virus has gone, the body can take a very long time to recover. Remember when you said I had to be patient? I'm trying. We all have to be patient. It's not easy, is it?"

I hugged her back. "No."

Two weeks on, and Mum *still* spent most of the time on the sofa, and Jonny and Sam *still* walked me to and from school. And now I had something else to worry about. Ever since the Milkshake Incident, my stomach hadn't been feeling right. It was as though there was something inside my tummy, wriggling around. Not all the time, but every now and then. It made me feel sick. After a while, it started to get in the way.

"It's football practice tonight," Mum said on Monday. "Sam said she'll take you again. That'll be good, won't it?"

I was going to say yes, I love footie practice, but suddenly my stomach gave a mighty lurch and I felt cold and sick. "Um," I said. "I don't think I want to go."

Mum stared at me, astonished. "You don't want to go? You've *never* said you don't want to go to football. Even when you had a fever of 40 degrees, you wanted to go. Even when you broke your ankle, you wanted to go."

I watched her pop a couple of pills out of a packet and swallow them without any water. My throat felt like it was closing up. I couldn't speak so I just shook my head.

"What's wrong?"

"I feel sick," I managed to croak out.

We sat on the sofa and watched a film together instead of me going out. But the horrible feeling in my stomach didn't go away. It kept twisting and turning all evening. And when I went to bed that night, I felt like there was a big spongy ball in my throat that I couldn't swallow. It made me panic. What was wrong with me?

Chapter 4

Slowly, very slowly, Mum did start to get better. It was such a relief to see her walk up and down stairs without gasping for breath, and she even started to walk me to school again, which was brilliant! The bad news was that I was feeling worse and worse and I didn't know why.

My teacher Miss Saliki asked me to stay behind one day.

"I'm worried about you, Harry," she said. "You used to be one of the bubbly ones in class, and now you hardly say a thing. I know your stomach hurts a lot. I think I'd better talk to your mum."

She did, and Mum made an appointment for the doctor. Nan took us because Mum was having a low-energy day and couldn't drive the car.

Doctor Kenrick asked me lots of questions about my tummy, and squidged it around a bit, which was weird, but I didn't mind too much. She also asked me if I'd been worrying about anything, so I told her about Mum being ill, and Mum explained a bit too.

Doctor Kenrick sat back and thought for a few moments. Then she said, "Well, there are a few things that could be causing your tummy ache and the horrible feeling in your throat, Harry. The first thing is an infection in your wee. We can test for that today. The second thing is that you might be developing a problem with some types of food. It would be worth keeping a diary of everything you eat for a couple of weeks, to see if the tummy ache could be linked to anything in particular. The third thing, which I think is probably the most likely, is that you're experiencing anxiety. Do you know what that means? It's when you worry about things so much that it interferes with your normal life. Anxiety can also cause headaches and tummy aches, as our tummy is our emotional centre."

By the time we left the doctor's room, my head felt very full of information, and Mum was clutching a bunch of leaflets.

"Poor Harry," she said, giving me a hug. "What a rotten time you're having. I suppose it's good that the infection test was clear at least."

"Anxiety?" said Jonny that evening at dinner. He looked at me. "Can't you just … I don't know, cheer up? I mean … life isn't *that* bad, is it?"

"Anxiety doesn't work like that, Jonny," said Mum.

And I thought, *why not? Why can't I just cheer up? He's right. And I feel all wrong.*

Chapter 5

There's a room at school called Rosie's Room. It's where kids can go if they're struggling. I'd never been before but Miss Saliki said it might be worth popping in to see Mr Atta who runs Rosie's. I'd seen Mr Atta around school and he was always friendly, so I went along one lunchtime and we played Connect 4. I won the first game easily which made me suspicious. "Did you lose on purpose?" I asked him.

He raised his hands. "I didn't, honestly. I'm no good at this game. I can beat you at Scrabble any day though."

"Oh," I said. "Would you rather play Scrabble then?"

"I don't mind losing," he said, with a big smile. "Do you know, I quite like it in a way. It takes the pressure off."

I hadn't thought of it like that before. So, we played a few more rounds and I won them all and he lost them all, and both of us were happy.

"How's your mum?" asked Mr Atta.

I shrugged. "All right. Getting better."

"Miss Saliki tells me you get tummy ache," said Mr Atta.

"Yes. The doctor thinks it's anxiety. I don't really know why though. I haven't got anything to be anxious about."

"How are you feeling about your mum ?"

"I was worried about her, but she's much better now. The tummy ache comes by itself. I'm not even thinking of anything."

"Do you like rollercoasters?"

"What?" I blinked.

"Rollercoasters." Mr Atta grinned at me. "Do you like them?"

"Uh. Yeah."

"So you know when you go on them, and they make your insides all get mixed up because you're going so fast, and your head gets dizzy, and you lose your breath, and your heart beats super-fast?"

"Yeah."

"When you get off the rollercoaster, all of those things you're feeling, they start to wear off, don't they? But for a few moments after the ride has finished, you're still dizzy and panting, and your insides are still swimming about, aren't they? I think maybe what's happening to you is like that."

I was really confused. "I haven't been on any rollercoasters."

He laughed. "No. But you went through a really scary time, didn't you? And maybe your body hasn't realised yet that the scary time is over and it's OK to relax. Anyway. Just a thought. Oh. Have you won again? Well done."

I went back to class
feeling thoughtful. We were
doing the Great Fire of London
and making collages with black
paper and orange and red tissue
paper for flames. I even forgot
about my stomach because I was
too interested in cutting out tiny
houses from black paper.

Miss Saliki went round
the class, looking at each pupil's
work and making suggestions
and giving compliments.
When she got to mine, she
exclaimed in delight. "Harry!
This is wonderful!" Before I could
say anything, she held it up
to show the rest of the class.
"Look, everyone! Look at
the detail Harry has put in his
houses – he's cut little windows
so we can see the flames
inside too. Excellent work, Harry."

It all happened so quickly. I felt a bit startled. Suddenly, everyone was looking at me. The big spongy ball expanded in my throat and I pressed my lips together because I was afraid I might throw up. Miss Saliki moved on to someone else and everyone looked away again, but I felt like I could hardly move. My body was cold and stiff. What was happening to me?

39

When we finally packed up at the end of the day, I almost ran to the playground. Seeing Mum there, sitting on a bench in her coat even though it was a warm day, made me burst into tears. I felt so embarrassed! I ran to her, threw my arms around her and buried my face in her coat so no one could see my face.

"Harry! What's the matter, what happened?"

But I didn't know what to tell her because *nothing* had happened! Mum tried to get me to talk on the way home, but I didn't know what to say. I just felt so stupid and tired and miserable and sick.

The next morning, my stomach started hurting from the moment I woke up. I stayed curled into a ball when Mum said it was time to get up.

"What's the matter, Harry?"

"I don't want to go to school."

"Is this about what happened yesterday?"

"Nothing happened yesterday. I just don't want to go in. I feel sick."

Mum rang the school and let me have the day off. But the thing is, the next day I felt exactly the same. I had another day at home. On the third day …

"Harry, you really must go in."

"I can't," I said, in a small voice. "I can't. Please don't make me."

I heard Mum on the phone to school. "I don't know what to do. Should I make him come in? He's so anxious."

When she came back, she said, "Mr Atta says how about you go in at lunchtime and spend the afternoon with him?"

I thought about this. I didn't really want to at all. I wanted to stay home, away from everyone, and maybe kick a ball around the garden. But I knew Mum wanted me to go into school. "I suppose," I said, in a small voice.

So I did, and it wasn't too bad. The next day I went in at lunchtime again, but this time, I had to go to class because Mr Atta was out doing some training. Miss Saliki turned to see me coming in with the others after break and said delightedly, "Harry, great to see you! I'm so glad you felt brave enough to come in today."

I wanted to shrivel into the ground. Everyone was staring at me again, and I heard someone say, "Brave? What does she mean, brave? I thought he was ill?"

My stomach hurt so badly, I asked to go home half an hour later. Then it was the weekend.

On Saturday morning, Mum said to me, "Harry, I've found something that might help."

"I don't think it will."

"You don't know what it is yet," she pointed out.

I sighed. We sat down together on the floor with our legs crossed. (Mum had her back against the wall so that it was less effort.) Then we closed our eyes. Mum switched on an app she'd downloaded, and this calm voice started to talk about breathing. We had to breathe in while the voice counted to four, and then hold it, and then breathe out slowly on another count of four.

To be honest, it was quite boring. Then the voice talked about noticing how our bodies were feeling, and what we could hear, and got us to imagine a happy place. Mine was a football pitch (obviously).

When the voice finished and I opened my eyes, I was quite surprised to find that 15 minutes had passed. Mum looked at me. "What did you think?"

"Er … it was all right." I wasn't sure what she expected me to say.

"How do you feel?"

"All right."

"I feel a bit calmer," she said. "Less worried."

"You're worried?" I repeated, surprised. "Do you have anxiety too?"

"You know, I think I might. I find it very hard to concentrate on anything at the moment. I keep thinking about things going wrong."

"You do?"

"And whether I'll ever have all my energy back." She pulled a face. "I don't like being like this, Harry."

I gave her a hug. "Well, if it helps you, then I'll do this with you every day to keep you company, and we can talk about how we're feeling afterwards."

She squeezed me back. "Thanks, Harry. You're the best."

Jonny stuck his head in the doorway. "I heard that."

"Mum," I said, later that day. "Why do I have anxiety and Jonny doesn't? He seems … fine."

"I don't know, Harry. Everyone is different. But – " she reached for my hand, "it's not your fault, Harry. Anxiety isn't something you made happen, and it's completely normal. We can help to manage it, I promise. There are lots of things we can do, but the key thing is that we all try to learn to understand ourselves better, open up to other people and share how we're feeling, and work together to challenge anything that's holding us back." She grinned at me. "A really wise person once said to me: 'One day at a time.'"

I squeezed her hand back. "And I'll help you manage your anxiety, too."

From then on, every morning we did the calming down app and talked to each other about how we felt, and over the next few days, I actually started to look forward to it. It was quite soothing, and I liked the fact that it was always the same. I knew what to expect, and it helped me to relax.

Don't get me wrong, my stomach still hurt, and I still had a spongy ball in my throat. The app wasn't magic. And I didn't make it into school much the following week, even though I tried. But … some things were nice.

Anxiety is hard to get rid of. I feel like something bad is about to happen all the time, and I have to stay at home where it feels safe. Miss Saliki gives me work to do at home, and Mr Atta checks in with me in a video call if I can't make it to school. I go into school three afternoons a week now, and next week I'll try to do four. Small goals, that's what Mr Atta says. Not trying to do everything at once. And sometimes I feel really anxious but I still manage to go in, and then I feel proud of myself.

Spending time with other people helps too. Zack, one of my friends, sometimes comes over to play football. He's in my team and he keeps trying to get me to come back to Monday practice.

"We need you, Harry. You're our best striker!"

"Maybe next week," I say.

Then one sunny morning, Mum is sitting in the garden watching me practise scoring, and she gets up and says, "Right, let's see you get past me." And even though she only stands in goal for two, maybe three minutes, it makes me so happy.

Maybe, if Mum can get better, I can too.

Maybe I *will* go to football practice next week. Fingers crossed.

Football is my favourite thing, after all.

53

Harry's anxiety

- How does Harry's anxiety change throughout the story?
- What helps Harry at each point to deal with his anxiety?

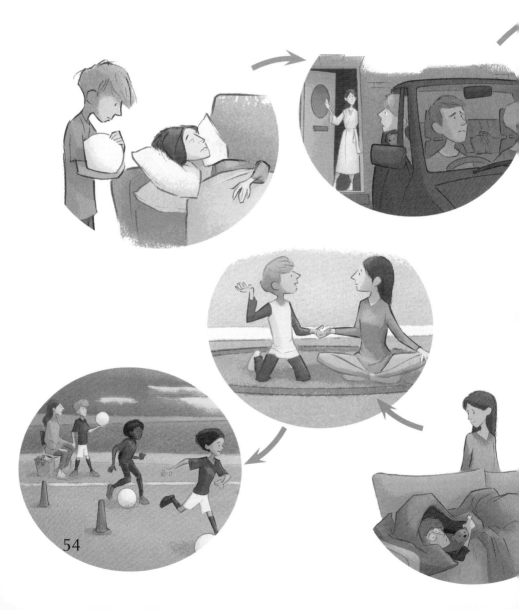

❧ Ideas for reading ❧

Written by Christine Whitney
Primary Literacy Consultant

Reading objectives:
- identify and discuss themes in a wide range of writing
- draw inferences such as inferring characters' feelings, thoughts and motives
- predict what might happen from details stated and implied
- explain the meaning of words in context
- identify main ideas drawn from more than one paragraph and summarise these
- provide reasoned justifications for their views

Spoken language objectives:
- participate in discussion
- speculate, hypothesise, imagine and explore ideas through talk
- ask relevant questions

Curriculum links: Science: Animals, including humans: recognise the impact of diet, exercise, drugs and lifestyle on the way bodies function

Interest words: anxiety, anxious, virus

Build a context for reading

- Ask children to explain the meaning of the word *anxiety* to the person next to them. There may be someone in the group who is prepared to share their experiences of anxiety. If so, allow them time to do so.
- Read the blurb on the back cover. Ask children to suggest ways in which Harry might get back to his usual self.
- Look at the front cover and notice the title. Encourage children to share their understanding of this.

Understand and apply reading strategies

- Read Chapter 1 together. Ask children to summarise what they know about Harry's family by the end of this chapter.
- Continue to read together up to the end of Chapter 2. Check children's understanding of the phrase *plugged into*. Ask children to explain the sequence of events that led to Harry saying, *I didn't think I'd ever want gingerbread flavour again.*